The Power
of an
Encouraging
Word

The Power of an Encouraging Word

Ken Sutterfield

New Leaf Press

ISBN: 0-89221-357-4
Library of Congress Catalog Number: 97-68953

Cover by Steve Diggs & Friends, Nashville, TN

Printed in the United States of America.

Please visit our website for other great titles:
www.newleafpress.net

For information regarding publicity for
author interviews contact
Dianna Fletcher at (870) 438-5288.

To the
diamond of my life

my wife,
Jan,

my biggest fan for over
twenty years.

Thank you for . . .
loving me
sharing with me
giving to me
honoring me

and
most of all . . .
for always encouraging me.

Acknowledgments

My deepest appreciation to:

Ragan and Spencer for being the best young men a dad could hope for.

John Lockhart for opening my eyes to the world of encouragement.

Dan Bolin for believing in me and providing me with tremendous opportunities.

Carl Wenger for the many times of "taking me to lunch" that were filled with affirmation and encouraging words.

Kyle Cochran, Mike Haigh, Sam Moreton, and Bill Wellons for blessing me with their friendship and encouragement.

My first family — thanks Dad, Mom, and Rita for all your love and encouragement

The staff, board and families of Ozark Conference Center for your faithful love and support.

Cecil Price of Christian Information Ministries International for his helpful research.

Tim Dudley and Jim Fletcher of New Leaf Press for seeing the vision of this project and encouraging me to go for it.

All the teachers, coaches, family, friends, and co-workers who have invested in my life with their words of encouragement.

Contents

Pleasant words to others can have a permanent, even eternal impact for good.

— Kenneth Parlin

Introduction

The Case for Encouragement

Encouragement . . . 1. To give courage, hope, or confidence 2. To help, give support; to be favorable; to foster: things that encourage.

The above definition from Webster's Dictionary rings true in my heart and soul. As I reflect on my life, turning points of encouragement mark my path. Parents, teachers, friends, co-workers, and family mark my life with words of encouragement.

As we consider the word "encouragement," we should heed the apostle Paul's words to the Hebrews. **"Encouraging one another; and all the more, as you see the day drawing near"** (Heb. 10:25). When we realize the value of mutual encouragement, consider the power unleashed and what could be accomplished. It is exciting to think that God has challenged us to encourage one another. The power of your encouraging words, spoken or written, could be the difference in the outcome of a single event or even one's life.

The great thing about encouragement is

that anybody can do it. You don't need a lot of time, money, or things. You don't even have to be a certain age to reach out and come alongside someone and elevate them to greater heights. However, what you do need is a willingness to put someone else's value above your own to give them hope and encouragement.

A good place to start is in our homes. That is where "actions are caught not taught." Children are like little sponges, waiting to soak up from their parents delight and encouragement. Let me challenge you to have a family that is different. Develop in your home a spirit of encouragement. You and your family will be forever grateful, and the encouragement modeled will continue for generations to come.

Dennis and Barbara Rainey, in their book *Building Your Mate's Self Esteem,* share a great lesson. "<u>Words are powerful seeds. Once planted, words will bring forth flowers or weeds</u>, health or disease, healing or poison. You carry a great responsibility for their use."[1] There is no denying that the words we speak do make a difference. The words we write will be remembered. As we look at the powerful partnership of words and encouragement, consider planting your own seeds of kindness to reap a world in bloom. "Therefore encourage each other with these words" (1 Thess. 4:18).

Few of us realize how much we need encouragement. Yet we must bask in the warmth of approval now and then or lose our self-confidence. All of us need to feel needed and admired. But unless we hear words of praise from someone else, how can we know that we are valued as a friend or co-worker?

A miracle happens to the person whose self-esteem has been raised. Praise is the polish that helps keep his self-image bright and sparkling. What does this have to do with giving a word of praise (encouragement)? You have the ability to perform that kind of miracle in another's life.

In a classic bit of advice, Lord Chesterfield suggested to his son that he follow the example of Duke de Nivernois: "You will perceive that he makes people pleased with him by making them first pleased with themselves."[2]

The effects of praise can be of great encouragement. A new pastor called to a church jokingly referred to as "the refrigerator" decided against criticizing his congregation for its coolness toward strangers. Instead, he began welcoming visitors from the pulpit and telling his congregation how friendly they were. Week after week he created the atmosphere of a friendly church, creating a picture of the church as he wanted it to be, giving his people a reputation to live up to. In time the congregation thawed. By encouraging and praising the ice-cube members they became warm-hearted human beings.

Encouragement helps rub off the sharp edges of daily contact. Nowhere is this more true than in marriage. Yet, it is in the home that the value of praise and encouragement is less practiced and appreciated. Children are especially hungry for praise, reassurance, appreciation, and encouragement. Take the time to find something positive to commend your child for and you will discover that both their ability and attitude improve. Words of encouragement are the most effective method of getting people to do their best.

As artists find the joy in giving beauty to others, so anyone who masters the art of encouragement through praising will find that it blesses the giver as much as the receiver. There are people everywhere in need of a good word, an uplifting compliment. The encouragement of others helps us move from fear to belief and action. Encouragement is the word, the note, the look that says, "I care about you. Yes, you can do it."

Encouragement is God-like. Scripture is full of promises about God's provision for us in times of difficulty. God reassures His people, "So do not fear, for I am with you; do not be dismayed, for I am your God. I will strengthen you and help you: I will uphold you with my righteous right hand" (Isa. 41:10).

Encouragement can make living in the midst of troubles easier. We need encouragement not just in crisis but in the midst of everyday life.

Two are better than one, because they have a good return for their work: If one falls down, his friend can help him up. But pity the man who falls and has no one to help him up! (Eccles. 4:9–10).

If you have ever been lifted up when you were suffering, you know the power of encouragement.
— Dr. Sinclair Ferguson

I'm convinced God uses encouraging words to strengthen our resolve to succeed. Dr. William Mayo of the Mayo Clinic used praise and encouragement with young doctors training at the clinic. One young doctor said, "You'd read a paper at a staff meeting and afterwards he'd see you in the elevator or the hall and would shake your hand or put his hand on your shoulder with a quiet 'Good work' and a straight warm look that made you know he meant it or perhaps a day or two later you'd get a note from him, saying, 'Dear _____, I learned more about _____ from that paper of yours the other night than I ever knew before. It was a good job.' Believe me, I prized those notes."[3]

Realizing that encouragement is of such great importance, William Barclay writes, "One of the highest human duties is the duty of encouragement. . . . It is easy to pour cold water on their enthusiasm; it is easy to discourage others. The world is full of discouragers. We have a Christian duty to encourage one another. Many a time, a word of praise or thanks or appreciation or cheer has kept a man on his feet."[4]

My hope and prayer for you as you read and reflect on these stories and encouraging words, is that they will become common place for you and in turn those you elevate, whether at home, in the work place, or with neighbors. There is truth in the saying, "Flowers leave part of their fragrance in the hand that bestows them." Won't you consider the power of your encouraging words and begin planting the seeds of kindness to reap a world in bloom?

Endnotes

1 Dennis and Barbara Rainey, *Building Your Mate's Self-Esteem* (Nashville, TN: Thomas Nelson Publishers, 1993), p. 104.

2 Gottfried R. von Kronenberger, *Signs of the Times* (Boise, ID: Southern Pub. Assoc., 1989).

3 Helen Clapesatte, *The Doctors at Mayo* (Minnesota University Press), p. 384.

4 William Barclay, *The Letters to the Hebrews, the Daily Study Bible* (Edinburgh: The Saint Andrews Press, 1955), p. 137-138.

Part I

The Healing Power of Words

Encouragement —

creating hope for the future.

— Ken Sutterfield

I Like It —
It's Kinda Cute

Haven't you longed for someone you care deeply for to encourage you? To tell you "You're great," to tell you "You're the best," "You're okay!" We need each other to encourage us, to give us hope in who we are. We want and we need to be accepted without a mask or veneer. We want to be loved apart from our performance or appearance. We deeply desire to be accepted, just as we are. Maurice Wagner writes "At the heart of personality is the need to feel a sense of being lovable without having to qualify for that acceptance."[1] We must choose our will . . . to accept unconditionally, just as Christ accepts us. Being an encourager requires intentionality. It may not come naturally. We need to recognize that we are all called to be encouragers, to build each other up, to bear each other's burdens, to sacrifice for others. God commands us to be encouragers. "But encourage one another daily, as long as it is called today, so none of you may be hardened by sin's deceitfulness" (Heb. 3:13).

Lois Moyday Rabey, who has personally experienced difficulty in her own life, writes, "Encouragement is not doing for someone what they can do for themselves. It is not removing pain from their lives. It is noticing them, feeling with them, and reminding them of the hope we have in Christ as we persevere in our walk with Him."[2]

We may think that because of our faith, difficulties, doubts, and discouragement should be easily overcome. But that isn't the case. Encouragement however can make living in the midst of those troubles easier.

For example, according to 1 Samuel 23:16-17, Jonathan, Saul's son, arose and went to David at Horesh and encouraged him in God. Thus, he said to him, "Do not be afraid, because the hand of Saul my father shall not find you, and you will be king over Israel and I will be next to you: and Saul my father knows this." Surely the anxiety and fear that David was experiencing was greatly relieved through the kind words of encouragement of his friend Jonathan.

In marriage, there is nothing so ugly as a husband and wife that attack each other with fierce barbs of disencouragement. But . . . nothing as beautiful as when words of encouragement are shared to lift the spirit and express love from a sacrificial heart. Many broken marriages have been restored through the healing power of words.

We each have a mental picture of those we

love and care for. But . . . what happens when that picture is broken and forever changed. When tragedy strikes, will you reflect love and acceptance or will you choose to be selfish and reject the one you once claimed to love? The following story illustrates how encouraging words and unconditional acceptance mirror a love so deep and pure.

Dr. Richard Selzer, in his book *Mortal Lessons: Notes in the Art of Surgery,* shares this beautiful story of how a loving relationship conforms to God's magnificent design. This is his story of seeing divinely inspired love up close:

I stand by the bed where a young woman lies, her face post-operative, her mouth twisted in palsy clownish. A tiny twig of the facial nerve, the one to the muscles of her mouth, has been severed. She will be thus from now on. The surgeon had followed with religious fervor the curve of her flesh: I promise you that. Nevertheless, to remove the tumor in her cheek, I had cut the little nerve.

Her young husband is in the room. He stands on the opposite side of the bed, and together they seem to dwell in the evening lamplight, isolated from me, private. *Who are they*, I ask myself, *he and this wry-mouth I have made, who gaze at and touch each other so generously, greedily?* The young woman speaks.

"Will my mouth always be like this?" she asks.

"Yes," I say, "it will. It is because the nerve was cut."

She nods, and is silent. But the young man smiles.

"I like it," he says. "It is kinda cute."

All at once I know who he is. I understand, and I lower my gaze. One is not so bold in an encounter with a god. Unmindful, he bends down to kiss her crooked mouth, and I so close can see how he twists his own lips to accommodate hers, to show her that their kiss still works. I remember that the gods appeared in ancient Greece as mortals, and I hold my breath and let the wonder in.[3]

Endnotes

1 Maurice Wagner, *The Sensation of Being Somebody* (Grand Rapids, MI: Zondervan Publishing House, 1975), p. 67.
2 Lois Mowdray, *Discipleship Journal,* Vol. 17 - No. 1, 1997.
3 Dr. Richard Selzer, *Moral Lessons: Notes in the Art of Surgery* (New York, NY: Simon & Schuster, 1976), p. 45-46.

Appreciation is thanking,

recognition is seeing, and

encouragement is bringing hope

for the future.

She Became My Mirror

Dr. Paul Brand writes of his experience as a surgeon in London, England, during World War II. He shares this story of how love casts out fear for a young pilot who received words that created hope, healing, and encouragement:

Peter Foster was a Royal Air Force pilot. These men [pilots] were the cream of the crop of England — the brightest, healthiest, most confident and dedicated, and often the most handsome men in the country. When they walked the streets in their decorated uniforms, the population treated them as gods. All eyes turned their way. Girls envied those who were fortunate enough to walk beside a man in Air Force blue.

However, the scene in London was far from romantic, for the Germans were attacking relentlessly. Fifty-seven consecutive nights they bombed London. In waves of 250, some 1,500 bombers would come each evening and pound the city.

The RAF Hurricanes and Spitfires that pilots like Foster flew looked like mosquitoes pestering the huge German bombers. The Hurricane was agile and effective, yet it had one fatal design flaw. The single propeller was mounted in front a scant foot or so from the cockpit, and the fuel lines snaked alongside the cockpit toward the engine. In a direct hit, the cockpit would melt off every feature of his face: his nose, his eyelids, his lips, often his cheeks.

These RAF heroes many times would undergo a series of 20 to 40 surgeries to re-fashion what once was their face. Plastic surgeons worked miracles, yet what remained of the face was essentially a scar.

Peter Foster became one of those "downed pilots." After numerous surgical procedures, what remained of his face was indescribable. The mirror he peered into daily couldn't hide the facts. As the day for his release from the hospital grew closer, so did Peter's anxiety about being accepted by his family and friends.

He knew that one group of airmen with similar injuries had returned home only to be rejected by their wives, who were unable to accept this new outer image of their husbands. Some men became recluses, refusing to leave their houses.

In contrast, there was another group who returned home to families who gave loving assurance of acceptance and continued worth. Many became executives and professionals, leaders in their communities.

Peter Foster was in that second group. His girlfriend assured him that nothing had changed except a few millimeters' thickness of skin. She loved *him*, not his facial membrane, she assured him. The two were married just before Peter left the hospital.

"She became my mirror," Peter said of his wife. "She gave me a new image of myself. Even now, regardless of how I feel, when I look at her she gives me a warm, loving smile that tells me I am okay," he tells confidently.[1]

Endnotes

1 Dr. Paul Brand and Philip Yancey, *In His Image* (Grand Rapids, MI: Zondervan Publishing House, 1984), p. 25-29.

Anxious hearts are heavy but a word of encouragement does wonders.

(Proverbs 12:25)

Committed to Encourage

In an age crippled by selfishness and an unwillingness to be committed to anything, we find ourselves as a society readily disposing of relationships like an old household product marketed for convenience when things get tough. The "C" word once stood alone but now has a companion — commitment and convenience respectfully have become words this society no longer truly understand.

The challenge for this generation is not to give over to convenience of disposable relationships, but rather to take a stand to be committed to take on the responsibility. Commitment creates hope for tomorrow and removes fear from our hearts.

Robert McQuilkin for many years was the president of Columbia Bible College in South Carolina. In 1981 McQuilkin's wife, Muriel, developed the first signs of Alzheimer's disease. For almost eight years McQuilkin lovingly carried on the responsibilities of president and loving husband. Then in March 1990, McQuilkin announced his resignation in a letter with these words of explanation, love, and encouragement.

My dear wife, Muriel, has been in failing mental health for about eight years. So far, I have been able to carry her ever-growing needs and my leadership responsibilities at CBC. But recently it has become apparent that Muriel is contented most of the time she is with me and almost none of the time I am away from her. It is not just "discontent." She is filled with fear — even terror — that she has lost me and always goes in search of me when I leave home. Then she may be full of anger when she cannot get to me. So it is clear to me that she needs me now full-time.

Perhaps it would help you to understand if I shared with you what I shared at the time of the announcement of my resignation in chapel. The decision was made, in a way, 42 years ago when I promised to care for Muriel "in sickness and in health . . . till death do us part." So, as I told the students and faculty, as a man of my word, integrity has something to do with it. But so does fairness. She has cared for me fully and sacrificially all these years; if I cared for her for the next 40 years I would not be out of debt. Duty, however, can be grim and stoic. But there is more; I love Muriel. She is a delight to me — her childlike dependence and confidence in me, her warm love, occasional flashes of that wit that I used to relish so, her happy spirit and tough resilience in the face of her continually distressing frustration. I do not have to care for her, I get to. It is a high honor to care for so wonderful a person.[1]

There is no doubt that McQuilkin knows the power of his presence and words do make a difference for his wife's encouragement. His sacrificial love certainly creates a new light to view the "C" words.

Endnotes
1 Dr. Robert McQuilkin, letter to Columbia Bible College, Columbia, South Carolina, 1990.

Correction does much, but encouragement does more. Encouragement after censure is as the sun after a shower.

— Johann Wolfgang von Goethe

My Mama's Words

Several years ago Dennis Rainey wrote a book challenging us to recognize the need to honor and give tribute to our parents. In an age when many adults are blaming their parents for what they did wrong and how they were victims of their parents' inadequacies, Rainey poses the question: "Have you ever honored your parents for what they did right?" We cannot argue the fact that no matter what age we are, we were commanded to "honor your father and mother."

The power of a written tribute will profoundly impact not only you but also your parents, children, and those around you.

On Mother's Day I sat in my church, Fellowship Bible Church, in Little Rock. Camile Richardson approached and stood at the podium. I have known or known about Camile for over 20 years. Her brother-in-law John Lockhart and Camile's sister Sharon had impacted me immeasurably as a college freshman working under their leadership at Lake Nixon Day Camp. John and Sharon were great examples of godly people to look to, trust in, and receive encouragement from.

Camile had been my link to the Lockharts for many years since they had long ago moved out of state. I also would often see Dr. and Mrs. Sawyer, Camile and Sharon's dad and mom occasionally. This family came from a long line of loving and encouraging people. I have attended cookouts at the Sawyer farm enjoying a touch of southern hospitality and a genuine love for God's people.

So as Camile began to speak on this Mother's Day, I was not just listening but I was seeing in full color, a living picture of the tribute to Mrs. Sawyer that Camile shared with us that day to help each one in the congregation recognize, honor, and encourage their own mothers. The following is the text of Camile's powerful words of encouragement paying tribute to her mom, Mary Sawyer:

Several years ago, before Jerry and I moved to Little Rock, I was attending a women's conference at our church. The lady who was leading it began by asking for an audience response to the question "What did your mother say?" There were the typical responses like "Stand up straight," and "Eat your vegetables." There were a couple of classics that I have remembered, which I know we all observe. "A lady only crosses her legs at the ankles and not the knees," and "Always carry a hanky in your hand and a dime in your shoe."

Do you know how many songs have been written about what our mothers have said? "Mama said there'd be days like this; there'd be days like this, my mama said." Or what about when Doris Day asked her mother if she'd be pretty or rich and her mother answered "Que sera, Que sera." I never did know if that meant she would be pretty and rich or poor and ugly. And of course there are the wise words of "My mama told me, you better shop around." My mama told me when I found Jerry, I better quit shoppin'.

And then there is Forrest Gump who pretty well lived his life by what Mama said.

I suppose I'm a lot like Forrest in that respect. My mom's words have had a profound impact on my life — and she's still talking and I'm still listening!

I remember her words — as she read the stories of the lives of missionaries to us four kids on our long vacations; as she quoted the second chapter of Luke every Christmas morning; as she sang hymns of faith at the piano. I remember her giving the gift of words to illiterate adults in our community as she taught them to read at our kitchen table.

One especially important day in my life I remember exactly what she said. I was a young single woman about to get on a plane and go 9,000 miles to the other side of the world to spend two years in Japan as a missionary. There were all kinds of thoughts and emotions going on in her and in me. Just as I was about to board she slipped me a note. I found my seat, sat down, and read these words: GOD'S WILL ONLY TAKES YOU WHERE HIS GRACE CAN KEEP YOU.

You know, she has said that to me hundreds of times since then — not verbally, but with her life. Sometimes it seems to me she's had more than her share of hard places in life. She has endured the pain of losing two sons, ages 16 and 28, entered that pain again when my sister lost a full-term son at birth, and then watched that same sister battle breast cancer. She has welcomed rebellious nieces and international students into her home when she had grown accustomed to life without teenagers. She has accepted unexpected changes and disappointments and done so with grace and strength.

My mom's words are loud and clear to me — His will takes you places where His grace keeps you.

What has your mama said? I hope you can take a moment today and remember — maybe to laugh, to cry, to be challenged or comforted — by her words. Maybe you can share that with her or with someone else. And I hope that those of us who are mothers are reminded of the awesome power in what we say!"

Yes! The power of an encouraging word will impact others for a lifetime. What kind of words are you using? Will they encourage or discourage? Words have a tremendous power — use them wisely.

Part II

Encourage One Another in "Community"

It is easily forgotten that the fellowship of Christian brethren is a gift of grace, a gift of the kingdom of God that any day may be taken from us, that the time that still separates us from utter loneliness may be brief indeed. Therefore, let him who until now has had the privilege of living a common Christian life with other Christians praise God's grace from the bottom of his heart. Let him thank God on his knees and declare: It is grace, nothing but grace, that we are allowed to live in community with Christian brethren.

— Dietrich Bonhoeffer
in *Life Together*

A Lesson from Geese

Each year as the seasons change and winter approaches, I look forward to seeing and hearing the geese as they migrate south in formation. Did you know as each goose flaps its wings it creates an "uplift" for the bird following? By flying in a "V" formation the flock as a whole adds 71 percent more flying range than if a bird flew alone.

We can certainly learn a lesson from this illustration from God's remarkable creation. People who share a common direction and a sense of community can get where they are going quicker and easier when they are traveling on the thrust of one another.

> Encourage one another; and all
> the more as you see the day drawing
> near (Heb. 10:25).

Also, when a goose falls out of formation, it suddenly feels the drag and resistance of trying to go it alone — and quickly gets back into formation to take advantage of the lift. We need to realize as Christians that we need to stay connected to one another, encouraging and helping each other. When the lead goose gets tired, it rotates back in the wing and another goose flies the point position.

Hebrews 4 includes an excellent passage for the encouragement of rest for God's leaders. The writer affirms the need to follow God's model for rest and encouragement.

> Let us therefore make every effort to enter that rest (Heb. 4:11).

Geese also honk from behind to encourage those up front to keep flying with speed.

Words are important. They have real power. James warns us that although the tongue is a small part of the body, it has the power to determine the whole course of human existence (James 3:5-6). What kind of message do you present when you "honk" at others?

Finally, another lesson we can learn is that when a goose is wounded or sick, two geese drop out of formation and follow their fellow member down to help and provide protection. They stay with this member of the flock until he or she is able to fly again or dies. Then they branch out on their own to catch up or join in another flock.

We, too, need to stand by one another — be a wind break in someone's life — a true encourager. By ourselves we are weak and fragile but together, with the Lord's strength, we can encourage one another with the power of our words.

It is astonishing what power words have over man.

— *Napoleon Bonaparte*

The Gift of Wonder

There was once an old monastery that had fallen upon hard times. Centuries earlier, it had been a thriving monastery where many dedicated monks lived and worked and had a great influence on the realm around. However, now there were only five monks who lived there. They were all over 70 years old. They were clearly a dying order. What would become of the monastery?

A few miles from the monastery lived an old hermit who many in the area believed was a prophet. One day as the monks came together they began agonizing over what seemed to be the impending demise of their order. One of them recommended that they should visit the hermit to see if he might have some advice for them. Perhaps he would be able to see the future and show them what they could do to save the monastery.

As they discussed it, they decided to make a visit to the hermit in his hut. They explained their dilemma and the purpose of their visit.

The hermit listened carefully but at the end he could only commiserate with them. "Yes, I understand," said the hermit. "The spirit has gone out of the people. Hardly anyone cares about old things any more." The abbot of the monastery asked, "Is there anything you can tell us that would help us save the monastery?"

"No I'm sorry," said the hermit. "I don't know how your monastery can be saved. The only thing that I can tell you is that one of you is an apostle of God."

The monks left the hermit's hut. They were both disappointed and confused by the hermit's cryptic statement. They returned to the monastery wondering what the hermit could have meant by the statement, "One of you is an apostle of God." For months after their visit, the monks pondered the power of the hermit's words.

One of us is an apostle of God. They wondered, *Did he actually mean one of us monks here at the monastery? That's impossible. We're all too old, too insignificant. On the other hand what if it is true? And if it's true, then which one of us is the apostle?* They began to question, *Do you suppose he meant Abbot? Yes, if he meant anyone, he most certainly meant Abbot. He has been our leader for more than a generation. Yet, on the other hand, he might have meant Brother Thomas. Certainly Brother Thomas is a holy man*

— a man of wisdom and light. He couldn't have meant Brother Elred, he gets crotchety at times and is difficult to get along with; however, he is almost always right. Maybe the hermit did mean Brother Elred. But surely he could not have meant Brother Phillip, for he is so passive, so very shy — a real nobody. However, he's always there when you need him. There is no doubt he's loyal and trustworthy. Yes, he could have certainly meant Phillip. Of course, he couldn't have meant me. I, for sure, am the most ordinary person in our order. Yet, suppose he did? Suppose I am the apostle of God? Oh Lord God, I couldn't be that much for You — could I?

As they contemplated in this manner, the old monks began to treat each other with extraordinary respect on the off chance that one of them might actually be an apostle of God. They began to encourage one another in ways that they had never ever even attempted.

The monastery was situated in a beautiful setting in the forest. Many people came there to picnic on its lawn and to walk on its paths and even now and then go into the chapel to pray and meditate. As they did so, without even being conscious of it, they sensed the aura of extraordinary respect, love, and encouragement that now began to surround the five monks and seemed to radiate from them, permeating the atmosphere of the entire place. There was something strangely attractive, even compelling about it. Hardly knowing why, people began to come back to the monastery more frequently to picnic, to play, and to pray. This place drew them and their friends.

Over time more and more visitors came, some of the younger men started to talk with the old monks. After a while one asked if he could join them. Then another and another. Within a few years the monastery had once again become a thriving order, and thanks to an old hermit's gift of words, a vibrant center of light and spirituality was saved and flourished throughout the realm.

If you want to change the world,

pick up your pen.

— *Martin Luther*

Shoebox Treasures

A dimly lit attic; dusty and hot. Stored away are all those priceless treasures too valuable to toss or donate to charity . . . boxed up memories, photos, memorabilia, and a shoebox full of treasures. As I opened the shoebox what should I find but priceless words of encouragement. Yes, I have found the treasure of words. As I open it I find the sparkle, glow, and glimmer of written notes, letters, and cards that I have collected for years. They're not in any order but I must have saved them for a reason. Why? Let's look inside and discover.

I know that you realize that God does many things in people's lives during weeks of family camp, but it would be easy for you to get distracted from the miracles happening around you because of the troubleshooting you must do as director. I just want to remind you that you are playing a key role in families' lives. Thanks for letting me be a part of your summer line-up.

Tim Kimmel

Just a note to tell you what an excellent job you are doing. You don't know how often I have recognized before God the gift He gave Ozark by directing you to be our director. It's a privilege to work with you.

Mike Haigh

Thanks for your encouragement and constant support. I know the Lord has really used you in my life.

Kay

I have never worked with someone that affected my life the way you have. Thank you for being such an encourager! I'm really going to miss you, Jan, and the boys. Thanks for the flowers and note. I hope your encouragement rubs off on me.

Rhonda

Thanks for your encouragement and may God bless you richly in the ministry.

Peb Jackson

Ken, thanks for your support, encouragement, and hugs this summer. You made a difference for me.

Crystal

Thank you for all you taught me last summer. You helped me to be honest about my struggles and fears. I grew a bunch. Thanks for your support.

Miriam

Well Ken, you have almost finished the summer. Congratulations! I've heard some really neat things and know you have really done a good job. I will continue to hold you up in my prayers.

Dan Dotson

Thank you so much for giving me the opportunity to work at Lake Nixon. I admire your work and you.

Ann

I appreciate all of your love and guidance this summer. I never thought I could be happy again. It's all because of God! I owe a lot to you for directing me in the right direction. It's true — God uses people every day. He certainly used you tremendously in my life. Thank you for being there!

Rebecca

Thanks for your confidence in having us come, and your sacrifice and encouragement to this speaker and his family. We appreciate you! Lord, bless you!

John & Cindy Trent

Ken, we are very proud of your work and we always want to participate with you in it.

Dad & Mom

I appreciate your encouragement and support of my decision. I am grateful for your support as we try to keep America free for all citizens.

> Mike Huckabee
> Governor of Arkansas

I just wanted to take the time to tell you how much I appreciate you. Your dedication to the Lord and to His ministry is really seen and I just wanted to say how much I appreciate your labor of love.

> June

I really praise the Lord for the friendship, leadership, and teacher that I've been blessed with by you! You do an awesome job!

> Sam

Great to have you in the studio — excellent job! Appreciate you!

> Dennis Rainey

Ken, your new job and added assignments looks like a good opportunity for you. You should be very proud of yourself because we're proud of you and for you.

We all will be coming down for Rita's [sister] pageant on April 7th. Ken, she needs your loving advice. We all need some encouragement, don't we?

> We love you lots!
> Dad

Ken — God is doing great things in you and through you. Don't be discouraged! I will stand with you no matter what comes our way. Together we will accept God's blessings and sufferings He allows because He is a loving God who is intimately at work for good in our lives. You have touched many lives over the years. God is using you! I love you.

Jan

Your notes and words of encouragement really helped me and kept me going. Know that I deeply respect you and your leadership. I am committed to follow your lead as long as you continue to follow Christ's lead. Ken, you are my friend. Be encouraged!

Your brother in Christ,
Kyle

These 20 excerpts from dozens of letters, notes, and cards that I have saved over the years are truly a treasure. These written words of encouragement brighten a cloudy day and allow the rays of sunshine to penetrate the dark days of life. Look in your attic or closet for your shoebox treasure. Your day will be full and bright as you read a word of encouragement.

A simple word

can renew hope.

— Lois Moyday Rabey

Kindness That Has No Price

For reasons long-forgotten a teenage girl got upset and angry with her parents and ran away to New York City. Cold, hungry, and friendless in a strange city, she was shivering on a street corner when a taxi pulled up. A group of people got out preparing to go to dinner. A man in the group noticed the girl. He approached her compassionately asking if she needed help and insisted that she join the group for dinner.

As they sat enjoying the meal together she told him her story. Later this man took the girl to the train station and bought her a ticket back home. Before she departed he shared some powerful words of encouragement with her. "Remember, whatever you desire, set your mind on it and the Lord will give you the desire of your heart. I know you'll be okay. You can do it." Then he gave her $20 and his address and telephone number. "If you ever need anything, please call."

The teenager returned to her family. Although she often thought of this man, she had lost the piece of paper with his name and number. Time went by and life improved for the girl. After graduation from high school, she attended college and then on to medical school and became a surgeon. Happily married, soon she was the mother of two children. Life had changed so much since that lonely time lost in the city. What a difference those words of encouragement had made in her life.

Some years later her own daughter, now a teenager, wanted to see some of her mom's vintage clothes for a school program. They went up to the attic to search through boxes and trunks. While looking, a diary was discovered and the lost piece of paper with the name and address was tucked inside.

Wanting to share with this kind benefactor what had transpired over these last 25-plus years, the mother, after months of inquires, located Mr. Ralf Burke. The woman sent a letter and a check for $300.00. She asked him to accept it with the love and spirit in which it was sent. The idea, she said "wasn't to repay a kindness that has no price," rather she hoped he would come meet her family and view what he had helped create by a simple act of kindness and words of encouragement.

Burke was welcomed like a long-lost uncle, insisting that we should all perform those simple acts of kindness and share words of encouragement to those we love and to those we don't even know. Their life impact is immeasurable![1]

Endnotes
1 Dorothy Willman, *Daily Progress*, Claremore, OK.

Plant a word of love heart-deep in a person's life. Nurture it with a smile and a prayer and watch what happens.

— Max Lucado

A Little Girl's Dream

The promise was a long time keeping. But then, so was the dream. In the early 1950s in a small southern California town, a little girl hefted yet another load of books onto the tiny library's counter.

The girl was a reader. Her parents had books all over their home, but not always the ones she wanted. She would make her weekly trek to the yellow library with the brown trim, the little one-room building where the children's library actually was just a nook. Frequently, she ventured out of that nook in search of heftier fare.

As the white-haired librarian hand-stamped the due dates in the ten year old's choices, the little girl looked longingly at *The New Book* prominently displayed on the counter. She marveled again at the wonder of writing a book and having it honored like that, right there for the world to see.

That particular day, she confessed her goal.

"When I grow up," she said, "I'm going to be a writer. I'm going to write books."

The librarian looked up from her stamping and smiled, not with the condescension so many children receive, but with encouragement.

"When you do write that book," she replied, "bring it into our library and we'll put it on display, right here on the counter."

The little girl promised she would.

As she grew, so did her dream. She got her first job in ninth grade, writing brief personality profiles, which earned her $1.50 each from the local newspaper. The money palled in comparison with the magic of seeing her words on paper.

A book was a long way off.

She edited her high school newspaper, married, and started a family, but the itch to write burned deep. She got a part-time job covering school news at a weekly newspaper. It kept her brain busy as she balanced babies.

But no book.

She went to work full-time for a major daily. Even tried her hand at magazines.

Still no book.

Finally, she believed she had something to say and started a book. She sent it off to two publishers and was rejected. She put it away, sadly. Several years later, the old dream increased in persistence. She got an agent and wrote another book. She pulled the other out of hiding, and soon both were sold.

But the world of book publishing moves slower than that of daily newspapers, and she waited two long years. The day the box arrived on her doorstep with its free author's copies, she ripped it open. Then she cried. She waited so long to hold her dream in her hands. Then she remembered that librarian's invitation, and her promise.

Of course, that particular librarian had died long ago, and the little library had been razed to make way for a larger incarnation.

The woman called and got the name of the head librarian. She wrote a letter, telling her how much her predecessor's words had meant to the girl. She'd be in town for her 30th high school reunion, she wrote, and could she please bring her two books by and give them to the library? It would mean so much to that ten-year-old girl, and seemed a way of honoring all the librarians who had ever encouraged a child.

The librarian called and said, "Come." So she did, clutching a copy of each book.

She found the big new library right across the street from her old high school, just opposite the room where she'd struggled through algebra, mourning the necessity of a subject that writers would surely never use, and nearly on top of the spot where her old house once stood, the neighborhood demolished for a civic center and this looming library.

Inside, the librarian welcomed her warmly. She introduced a reporter from the local newspaper — a descendant of the paper she'd begged a chance to write for long ago.

Then she presented her books to the librarian, who placed them on the counter with a sign of explanation. Tears rolled down the woman's cheeks.

Then she hugged the librarian and left, pausing for a picture outside, which proved that dreams can come true and promises can be kept. Even if it takes 38 years. The ten-year-old girl and the writer she'd become posed by the library sign, right next to the reader-board, which said: WELCOME BACK, JANN MITCHELL.[1]

Endnotes

1 Jann Mitchell, Heath Communications, Inc. 3201 SW 15th Street, Deerfield Beach, FL 33442, 1994.

Encouragement, for persistent
faithfulness in the small task:

No matter if your jobs are small,
And your rewards are few:
Remember that the mighty oak
Was once a nut like you.

— Author unknown

That's the Way We Do Things

Laura Ricad tells a story of a young man and his encounter with a Vermont couple and their profound impact on his life. It all started when this young man had left his car parked while he was hiking. On his return he found a dent in his car and a note tidily written. "We'll be waiting for you" with a phone number.

The memory of our encounter in their farmhouse kitchen, as we exchanged insurance information, has never left me. To my thanks he said simply "That's the way we do things," while his wife, beside him, dried her hands on her apron and smiled. *"That's the way we do things."*

Over many years his words often came back to me. Theirs were lives of decency and order. What was their secret, I wondered? I resolved that one day I would see them again.

One day I headed for southern Vermont with a homemade lattice-top rhubarb pie on the seat beside me.

Struggling to remember where they lived, I drove to the park. I described their farm to a ranger there — dwarf apple trees by an old stone barn, a field full of sunflowers, hollyhocks, and foxgloves massed in beds just before the farmhouse door. He grinned at me. Most of this state looks like that, unless you can give me something else — a name. . . . I couldn't.

Hours later after looking but not finding them, I pulled into a picnic area, a grove of beautiful huge white pines set next to a cold stream. I admitted to myself that my mission had come to nothing.

"Excuse me," a stranger said. He had locked his keys in his trunk. "Would you please phone a locksmith for me or possibly give me a ride into town?"

His wife introduced herself and told me that her husband was a botanist, recently retired from a small college in Pennsylvania, and that they were traveling north to collect ferns. As we drove, she looked out the window and he botanized all the way into Chester, pointing out black-eyed susans along the roadside.

While the locksmith worked, the botanist and his wife and I sat around the picnic table and shared my rhubarb pie. "My uncle used to say it was bad luck to plant rhubarb in a place you didn't plan to make a home."

I related my story and my mission and how

it had failed. "Not by our lights" he replied, patting his stomach and jangling his keys.

"You've been very kind" his wife said sweetly. "Nowadays not too many people. . . ."

I realized then what had taken place and waved off her comment. "That's the way I do things," I said simply realizing the magic and impact of those encouraging words in my own life.[1]

Endnotes
1 Laura Ricad, *Yankee*, Dublin, NH, June 1995.

A soothing tongue is a
tree of life.

— Proverbs 15:4

Go West? — Yes!

Ever since his days in Congress, Thomas Jefferson showed great interest in western expansion. The Louisiana Purchase ranks as one of Jefferson's greatest achievements. The Louisiana Territory was a vast region between the Mississippi River and the Rocky Mountains. In fact, it was Jefferson who had the vision and initiated the expedition of Lewis and Clark, the great explorers.

Another interesting fact about Jefferson was that he was the first president to write out and send Congress his annual message rather than deliver it in person. Jefferson was not known as a great speaker, so to assure that he would be able to communicate his interests with passion he chose to write them out. He understood the power of written words and their lasting impact.

A story is told about Thomas Jefferson and a group of companions who were traveling across country on horseback. They came to a river which had left its banks because of a recent downpour. The swollen river had washed the bridge away. Each rider was forced to ford the river on horseback, fighting for his life against the rapid currents. The very real possibility of death threatened each rider, which caused a traveler who was not part of their group to step aside and watch. After several had plunged in and made it to the other side, the stranger asked President Jefferson if he would ferry him across the river. The president agreed without hesitation. The man climbed on, and shortly thereafter the two of them made it safely to the other side.

As the stranger slid off the back of the saddle onto dry ground, one in the group asked him, "Tell me, why did you select the president to ask this favor of?" The man was shocked, admitting he had no idea it was the president who had helped him. "All I know," he said, "is that on some of your faces was written the answer 'No,' and on some of them was the answer 'Yes.' His was a 'Yes' face." A face of encouragement.

What kind of face do you have? Does your face say . . . Yes? Keep on keeping on — You can do it — I love you no matter what — *Be encouraged* — I'm here with you.

Make a face — a face of encouragement.

Part III

Changed Lives

Real encouragement occurs when words are spoken from a heart of love.

— Dr. Larry Crabb

YMOT! A Changed Life!

As an organization matures it needs to have all kinds of individuals, each one of whom is dedicated to bringing out the best in the other individual and using their strengths. You can't change your personality but you can change your behavior in significant ways so you can fit into a team. You shouldn't try to change your personality because your personality is a gift.

The greatest leaders that I have known in both the corporate world and the Christian world are the people who can reach into the hearts and minds and lives of other people and bring out the very best in them and build on their strengths.

I'd like to tell you a story about a person I knew who I think was probably the best at this of anyone I've ever known. She was not an executive, a manager, a leader or an author, or anybody you've ever heard of. She was an old-fashioned school teacher. This woman was old-fashioned!

She came to school in a white blouse and

a black skirt, not blue mind you, but black, and she had black shoes that laced up. She was always absent one day a semester and we all assumed that was the day she got her skirt cleaned. She had gray hair which she combed once a month whether it needed it or not. There were only a few things that Nettie Weidenmann loved. She loved children. She *loved* children; the most precious resource in the world, our children. Invest your life in children and it will never be a wasted life. The second thing that she loved was learning and growth and development. She loved both of those.

She had a great impact on a young man who was a friend of mine. When he went to school he discovered that he had a problem. The first thing you have to do when you go to school is learn to write your name. He picked up the pen after he'd mastered some letters and he wrote his name. In those days he was called Tommy by everybody and he wrote his name "ymot," with the "y" turned around backwards, one "m" dropped out, and the whole thing scrambled backwards.

The teacher that he had in first — not Nettie Weidenmann — was very impatient with this behavior. In fact about the second or third week of school she came over and she said, "If you don't quit that clowning around I'm going to start calling you 'YMOT!' "

Well, it was one of those nicknames that caught on fast. The kids couldn't wait until recess to start calling him Ymot. "Hey, Ymot! Throw a ball over here, Ymot." Everybody started calling him Ymot. Relatives called him Ymot, teachers called him Ymot, new kids came to school and thought his name was Ymot.

In addition to that, he had a pretty short attention span and was very hyperactive. So you can imagine what his spelling and math papers looked like. He'd try for two or three minutes, give up in despair, crawl around the back of the room, raise Cain, give them trouble. Actually, for three years he spent very little time in class. He spent most of his time on a chair out in the hall which came to be known as "Ymot's chair." In fact, other children when they were punished were told to go sit on Ymot's chair, like he was leasing it out to them for half an hour or so.

After three years the school had had enough of this. They sent the most interesting note home to Ymot's parents. It said, "Please do not send Ymot back to this school in the fall. (Would you believe the school even used the nickname?) They said, "You must face the fact that your son will never finish a normal elementary school. You must face the fact that he is severely retarded and get him into a special program." The letter went on to make some suggestions about programs they could get him into. But Ymot's parents had a big problem with that note. They couldn't read it either because they weren't elementary school graduates.

The following fall they did the only thing they knew how to do . . . they sent him back to this little neighborhood school. That was when he had Nettie Weidenmann. About the second week of school Nettie Weidenmann said, "I want you to stay in at recess. **I have something very important to tell you**." Did you ever have a teacher like that? Every time they spoke it was like Moses! After the rest of the kids had gone she came back and she sat in the little chair next to Ymot's desk and she said, **"I have something important to tell you. You have a WONDER-FUL mind!"**

He said, "You want to run that by me one more time? Have you seen my record?" She said something he didn't appreciate until many years later.

She said, "No! I never look at a student's previous record. **It doesn't mean a thing! They haven't had ME yet!**" Isn't that great?? She said, "Here's what we'll do. We'll take half an hour at one of the two recesses per day, half an hour at lunch, and an hour after school. That's going to be two hours a day and you and I will be buddies and we're going to practice." Every day she would begin the session by saying, "You have a good mind. You can do great things. You can accomplish significant things."

The deal was that if he could write his name six times out of ten by the end of the semester, he'd get an "A" on every subject. Well, he failed in that objective, but as the second semester began she said, "I'll tell you what, I noticed something about you. You don't live very far from me. Why don't you come over to my house on Saturday?" Can you imagine a teacher that would do that for a student after spending five days with him?

There were Saturdays when it went well and there were Saturdays that it went so badly that he'd pound his head on the table in her kitchen until it was red. At the end of the second semester, guess what? He achieved his goal! He surpassed his goal. He could write his name nine times out of ten. Not just the first name but the last name and many other words, and he got an "A" on every subject.

The following year he came back to the fifth grade and he walked in and thought he must have made another dumb mistake. Standing at the front of the fifth grade was Nettie Weidenmann. I'll tell you something interesting. She taught school in this little neighborhood place for 40 years. Thirty-nine years she taught the fourth grade. One year only she taught the fifth grade and I never knew why. What I can tell you is that everything that I have ever accomplished in my life, I owe on a human level to my fourth and fifth grade teacher, who was Nettie Weidenmann, because I'm sure you have guessed by now, Ymot was not my friend, but me.

When I was about 14 years of age, I resumed my habit of going back to visit her on Saturdays. She was retired and she was losing her eyesight. I remember one time I said, "Miss Weidenmann, why did you spend so much time with me? Did you just love all of your students?"

She just lit up like a bright light and said, "Oh yes! I loved all my students but that's not why I spent so much time with you. What I want you to understand is that most of all I love my Heavenly Father and His Son Jesus Christ. My life is a fulfillment of my mission to which I committed myself as a Christian."

Well I had never heard about things like that before. I kept going back Saturday after Saturday. Finally, this woman who had led me into my future, who had led me into my self, led me into the kingdom of God.

That happens all the time in public schools and in private schools. It happens in families, it happens in organizations. Positive reinforcement is not a gimmick. It's the most dynamic thing that can happen between two people, where one says to the other, "I have high expectations, I believe in you, I'm going to demand a lot, it's not going to be easy but I'll be with you every step of the way to help you grow and help you develop. That is leadership![1]

Endnotes
1 Thomas J. Stevenin, Moody Broadcasting Network, 820 N. LaSalle Blvd., Chicago, IL 60610-3284.

A word fitly spoken is like apples of gold in a setting of silver.

— Solomon

Three Letters from Teddy

Teddy Stallard certainly qualified as "one of the least" — disinterested in school; musty, wrinkled clothes; hair never combed: one of those kids in school with a deadpan face; an expressionless, glassy, unfocused stare. When Miss Thompson spoke to Teddy he always answered in monosyllables. Unattractive, unmotivated, and distant, he was just plain hard to like.

Even though his teacher said she loved all in her class the same, down inside she wasn't being completely truthful. Whenever she marked Teddy's papers, she got a certain perverse pleasure out of putting X's next to the wrong answers, and when she put the F's at the top of the papers, she always did it with a flair. She should have known better; she had Teddy's records and she knew more about him than she wanted to admit. The records read:

> 1st Grade: Teddy shows promise with his work and attitude, but poor home situation.

2nd Grade: Teddy could do better. Mother is seriously ill. He receives little help at home.

3rd Grade: Teddy is a good boy but too serious. He is a slow learner. His mother died this year.

4th Grade: Teddy is very slow, but well-behaved. His father shows no interest.

Christmas came and the boys and girls in Miss Thompson's class brought her Christmas presents. They piled their presents on her desk and crowded around to watch her open them. Among the presents was one from Teddy Stallard. She was surprised that he had brought her a gift, but he had. It was wrapped in brown paper and was held together with Scotch tape. On the paper were written the simple words, "For Miss Thompson from Teddy." When she opened Teddy's present, out fell a gaudy rhinestone bracelet, with half the stones missing, and a bottle of cheap perfume.

The other boys and girls began to giggle and smirk over Teddy's gifts, but Miss Thompson at least had enough sense to silence them by putting on the bracelet and putting some of the perfume on her wrist. Holding her wrist up for the other children to smell, she said, "Doesn't it smell lovely?" And the children, taking their cues from the teacher, readily agreed with "oohs" and "aahs."

At the end of the day, when school was over and the other children had left, Teddy lingered behind. He slowly came over to her desk and said softly, "Miss Thompson, you smell just like my mother . . . and her bracelet looks real pretty on you, too. I'm glad you liked my presents." When Teddy left, Miss Thompson got down on her knees and asked God to forgive her.

The next day when the children came to school, they were welcomed by a new teacher. Miss Thompson had become a different person. She was no longer just a teacher; she had become an agent of God. She was now a person committed to loving her children and doing things for them that would live on after her. She helped all the children, but especially the slow ones, and especially Teddy Stallard. By the end of the school year, Teddy showed dramatic improvement. He had caught up with most of the students and was even ahead of some.

She didn't hear from Teddy for a long time. Then one day, she received a note that read:

Dear Miss Thompson:
    I wanted you to be the first to know. I will be graduating second in my class.
                Love, Teddy Stallard

Four years later, another note came:

Dear Miss Thompson:

They just told me I will be graduating first in my class. I wanted you to be the first to know. The university has not been easy, but I liked it.
Love, Teddy Stallard

And four years later:

Dear Miss Thompson:

As of today, I am Theodore Stallard, M.D. How about that? I wanted you to be the first to know I am getting married next month, the 27th to be exact. I want you to come and sit where my motheR would sit if she were alive. You are the only family I have now; Dad died last year.
Love, Teddy Stallard

Miss Thompson went to that wedding and sat where Teddy's mother would have sat. She deserved to sit there; she had done something for Teddy that he could never forget.[1]

Endnotes

1 Elizabeth Silance Ballard, *Home Life,* The Sunday School Board of the Southern Baptist Convention.

Pleasant words are a
honeycomb . . . sweet to the
soul and healing to the bones.

— *Proverbs 16:24*

Words in a Wallet

Sister Helen Mrosla taught ninth grade math for many years at Saint Mary's school in Morris, Minnesota. One Friday when her class became frustrated and edgy with one another due to the difficulty of an exercise, she knew this crankiness had to stop before it got out of hand. Sister Helen had each pupil write the names of each student in the room on two sheets of paper, leaving a space between each name. Then she instructed the class to write the nicest thing they could think of about that person. That Saturday, she wrote down the name of each student on a separate sheet of paper, and listed all the nice things that were said about them. On Monday she gave each student his or her sheet with all the comments said about them. Each student was thrilled to see all that was said.

Before long, the whole class was smiling. You could hear whispered across the room: "Wow!" "Really!" "I never knew that meant anything to anyone!" "I didn't know others liked me so much!"

No one mentioned those papers again. The

exercise accomplished its purpose. The students were happy with themselves and one another again.

Several years went by when Sister Helen received the news that one of her former students, Mark Eklund, had been killed in Vietnam. She remembered him well. Mark had been in Sister Helen's very first class while in the third grade. Mark was one in a million. He had that happy-to-be-alive attitude that made even his occasional mischievousness delightful. Mark was also in one of Sister Helen's ninth grade math classes.

Sister Helen received a phone message from the Eklund's family that day requesting that she attend Mark's funeral. The church was packed with Mark's friends. They sang "The Battle Hymn of the Republic." The pastor said the usual prayers and the bugler played taps. One by one those who loved Mark took a last walk by his coffin.

Sister Helen recalls "I was the last one. As I stood there, one of the soldiers who acted as a pallbearer came up to me."

"Were you Mark's math teacher?" he asked. I nodded as I continued to stare at his coffin. "Mark talked about you a lot." he said.

After the funeral Mark's mother and father were waiting to see Sister Helen. "We want to show you something," Mark's father said, taking a wallet out of his pocket. "They found this on Mark when he was killed. We thought you might recognize it."

Sister Helen opened the billfold, carefully removing two worn pieces of notebook paper that had obviously been taped, folded, and re-folded many times. "I knew without looking that the papers were the ones on which I had listed all the good things each of Mark's classmates had said about him."

Soon Mark's classmates started to gather around. Charlie smiled rather sheepishly and said "I still have my list, too. It's in my top desk drawer at home."

"I have mine, too" said Marilyn. "It's in my diary."

Then Vickie, another classmate, reached into her pocketbook, took out her wallet, and showed her worn and frazzled list, also. "I carry this with me at all times. I think we all saved our list."

Yes, words do matter and their impact may never be fully realized. Encouraging words have a lasting effect. Never underestimate the power of an encouraging word.[1]

Endnotes
1 Helen P. Mrosla, *Proteus*, Shippensburg University, Shippensburg, PA 17257, 1991.

*We live by encouragement
and we die without it, slowly,
sadly, and angrily.*

— Celeste Holme

Encouraged to Dream

My family and I moved to Tyler, Texas, in January 1984 to begin our ministry at Pine Cove Conference Center. One of the first families we met were the Peels. Bill was the pastor of a new growing church fellowship and Kathy was a homemaker with two boys, John and Joel, just a few years older than our sons, Ragan and Spencer. We enjoyed occasional times together during our seven years in Tyler.

During that time we observed Bill and Kathy as they worked with and trained their boys (now three with the addition of James), realizing that our own sons would soon be where John and Joel were in their development. However, the most interesting observation we made of the Peel family was not of their boys but their mom, Kathy.

It all began in 1987 at a retreat in East Texas where Bill was the retreat speaker. Kathy, attempting to be the attentive wife, listened as Bill encouraged the group to take their dreams seriously and discover God's design for their life. As Bill spoke, his words struck a responsive chord, Kathy recalls. It was Psalm 37:4-6 "Delight yourself in the Lord and he will give you the desires of your heart. Commit your way to the Lord; trust in him and he will do this: He will make your righteousness shine like the dawn, the justice of your cause like the noonday sun."

"I sat mesmerized as Bill suggested that if we are people who want to delight ourselves in the Lord, people who want to please and obey God, then the desires of our heart may have been placed there by God for a reason. The very dreams within us could be keys to understanding why God put us here on planet Earth at this particular time in history. In other words, Bill asked us to believe, even if we could believe only with poppy-seed-sized faith, that God plants His desires in His people.

"Then Bill gave us an assignment. He asked each of us to go off somewhere and write down the ten most wonderful things God could do for us for the rest of our life — the dreams or desires that we've always wanted to pursue. He instructed us not to let anything limit our dreams — not education, finances, location, age, or any kind of circumstances. We were just to permit ourselves to think about what we would really like to do if there were nothing holding us back." Kathy remembers her embarrassment at the thought of sharing her dreams openly. But . . . Bill had encouraged her to dream with no limitation.

Dream #1: To write a book that will encourage women.

Dream #2: To speak to large groups of women encouraging them to learn God's truths.

The retreat ended and the Peels returned home to Tyler with all the real world responsibilities of laundry, cooking, grocery shopping, and yes, bills.

One Saturday six weeks later, Kathy handed Bill his usual "honey do" list, only this time there was a special request added — "Publish a Book"! With shock and surprise Bill questioned Kathy about this unusual request. Kathy responded with, "Now look, you got me into this. I'm just following your advice and getting in touch with the dreams and desires within my heart."

After months of planning, praying, and some two thousand dollars, Kathy and fellow mom Joy Mahaffey wrote, edited, chose art work, and laid out the first self-published edition of *A Mother's Manual for Summer Survival.*

The date was March 31, 1988. This was just the beginning of a dream realized for Kathy. Bill's words of encouragement and God's gentle whisper began a new work in Kathy as she pursued the dreams that God had put in her heart.

A Mother's Guide to Summer Survival has sold over 350,000 copies and is now published by Focus on the Family.

What started as a seed of faith germinated with a word of encouragement and is now reaping a world in bloom. The magnitude of Bill's encouraging words to Kathy are still unfolding.

Since that retreat in 1987, Kathy Peel has authored 12 best-selling books which have sold 1.2 million copies. She is editor-in-chief of *Family Manager* magazine, serves on the staff of *Family Circle* magazine and has written for numerous other publications. Kathy has appeared on over 350 TV and radio programs and speaks frequently nationally and internationally.

What is your dream?

What have you been encouraged to consider? What is the desire of your heart? God is big enough and cares enough to help you discover His plan for you. I encourage you to discover how God is going to use you for His kingdom.

God spoke and the world was created. Consider the power of HIS encouraging words.[1]

Endnotes

1 Bill and Kathy Peel, *Discover Your Destiny* (Colorado Springs, CO: Navpress, 1996), p. 52-54.

Part IV

Sports Victories

The heart of a fool is in his
mouth, but the mouth of a wise
man is in his heart.

— Benjamin Franklin

It's Just Halftime

Jerry Clavelle, a longtime coach in the NFL, including the Houston Oilers and the Atlanta Falcons, shares that there are at least 20 qualities of leadership within any organization. However, of these 20-plus there are two that stand out for character and anti-discouragement.

The Falcons were playing the Pittsburg Steelers on their home turf in Pittsburgh. It was a tough game and the team had a sense that they had hit the wall.

During the first half, Pittsburgh led 3-0. With just a few seconds left on the clock in the first half, Atlanta had the ball on Pittsburgh's one yard line. The conventional wisdom was to kick a field goal and go into the locker room with an even score.

The coach, Clavelle, had another idea. The quarterback called a play from the line of scrimmage, an end run to the left. As the play began, the Steelers just happened to all flow the same direction and therefore easily stopped the Falcons for a seven-yard loss.

A strong sense of discouragement came over the entire Falcon team as they left the field at halftime, still down by three. A huge defensive lineman muttered to himself under his breath, "Stupid coach, dumb play." All the way through the tunnel leading to the locker room the defensive lineman continued, " Stupid coach, dumb play." The whole team seemed to have the same feeling.

In the locker room, the team divided for their second-half strategy. One board was in front of the defense, and another board was in front of the offense. The defensive lineman still was muttering but with greater intensity: "Stupid coach, dumb play!" About that time, a running back of considerably smaller physique approached the lineman, "What did you say?"

The lineman stood up and looked the running back straight in the eye. "I said, stupid coach, dumb play." With frustration building and with a determined spirit, the running back slugged the lineman and knocked him out cold. "Don't talk about our coach or our plays. It's just halftime."

Though the lineman was knocked out and did not play the second half, the team was encouraged by the determination and attitude of the running back to be persistent and to encourage each other rather than discourage. The team won the game 30-13!

All of us need people around us with anti-discouragement. We live in a day where the "naysayers" and "I told you so's" hold us back. Don't give way to the words of discouragement but rather to the power of words that create hope and perseverance.

Wise sayings often fall on barren ground; but a kind word is never thrown away.

— Sir Arthur Helps

24-Carat Friendship

Jesse Owens seemed sure to win the long jump at the 1936 Olympic games in Berlin, Germany. Just the year before he had set three world records in one single day. He was the record holder for the running broad jump with 26 feet 8-1/4 inches — a record that would stand for 25 years.

As he walked to the long jump pit, however, Owens saw a tall, blue-eyed, blond German taking practice jumps in the 26 feet range. Owens was nervous. He was aware of the tension created with his presence. He knew the Nazi's desire was to prove "Aryan superiority," especially over the blacks.

The pressure was overwhelming and on his first jump Owens inadvertently leaped from several inches beyond the takeoff board. Rattled, he fouled on his second attempt, too. He was only one foul away from being eliminated.

At this point, the tall German approached Owens and introduced himself as Luz Long. "You should be able to qualify with your eyes closed!" he said to Owens, referring to his two earlier jumps.

Then an amazing event took place. The black son of a sharecropper and the white model of Nazi manhood chatted in view of the entire stadium. What were they talking about?

Since the qualifying distance was only 23 feet 5 1/2 inches, Long suggested making a mark several inches before the takeoff board and jumping from there, just to play it safe. Amazing! At the beginning of World War II, this model of Germany's strength was providing technical assistance and words of encouragement to a foe both on and off the field.

As you might imagine, Owens qualified easily. In the finals, Owens set an Olympic record and earned the second of four gold medals during the 1936 Olympics. The first person to congratulate Owens was Luz Long — in full view of Adolf Hitler.

Owens never saw Long again, who was killed in World War II. What did Jesse Owens think of Luz Long and his words of encouragement? "You could melt down all the medals and cups I have," Owens later wrote, "and they wouldn't be plating on the 24-carat friendship I felt for Luz Long."

Simple but impacting words make a difference that lasts a lifetime.

We make a living by what we get, but we make a life by what we give.

— Winston Churchill

Get Out There and Play

In 1929, on New Years Day, the Rose Bowl game between Georgia Tech and the University of California was underway. Roy Reigels played for Cal. In the first half of the game, Roy delivered a bone-crushing tackle on the Georgia Tech tailback. Although the tackle shook Roy up a bit, it separated the ball from the arms of the runner and Roy was able to scoop up the ball, turn and begin a 90-yard sprint toward the goal line. The fans were screaming, Roy's adrenaline was pumping, and he ran as hard as he could until he was finally tackled from behind on the two-yard line. Wow! What a run!

But when Roy looked up to face his tackler, he found himself staring into the face of his own teammate. You see, having been dazed when he hit the tailback, Roy lost his sense of direction on the field. He had returned the ball 90 yards toward his own goal line. The crowd and his teammates were either stunned or livid with anger. On the next play, the defense stuffed

Cal in their own end zone, causing a safety, and two points for Georgia Tech. From that day on, Roy has been known as "Wrong Way Reigels."

But that is just the beginning of the real story. It centers around what happened at half-time that day. As you can imagine, the players had very little to say as they lumbered into the locker room. The Cal coaching staff was even more stunned than the players. The head coach, who usually took full advantage of the time to make connections, encourage, and inspire, sat silently on a chair in front of the team. The only sound was the weeping of Roy Reigels who had collapsed in the corner and buried his dirty face in his hands.

Soon the referee stuck his head in the door and shouted, "Three minutes, Coach!" The coach remained silent for a moment. Everyone was wondering, "What will he do about Reigels?" "What is he going to say to Roy?" Eventually the coach stood up and said, "The same 11 who started the first half will start the second." The team jumped up from their benches and went to take the field. All except Roy, that is. Roy just sat in the corner and cried.

"Reigels!" said the head coach. "Didn't you hear me, boy? Get up and on the field." Roy just sat there sobbing even harder. Then the coach walked over to where Roy was sitting, knelt down in front of him, and said softly,

"Roy, I said the same team that started the first half is starting the second. We need you, man. Get out there and play."

Roy looked up and said through his tears, "I can't, Coach. I let you down and I let the team down. I've ruined the game and embarrassed myself and our school. I can't go back out there now!"

I don't know what you would have said if you had been that boy's coach. But the next words that came out of this wise man's mouth should be recorded in the Hall of Fame. He gently reached down under Roy's chin, lifted his face so he could look him in the eyes, and said, "Roy, the game is only half over . . . now get out there and play."

Do you know of someone you need to come alongside of and encourage to "get out there and play"? The game of life is NOT over!

History has demonstrated that the most notable winners usually encountered heartbreaking obstacles before they triumphed. They won because they refused to become discouraged by their defeats.

— B. C. Forbes

The Finish Line

Every four years, amateur athletes from nations throughout the world compete in the Olympic games. No other sports spectacle has such an historic or thrilling background. Flags flutter from the top of a crowd-filled stadium. Cheers from around the world ring out as the runner enters the stadium carrying the Olympic torch. The lighted torch has been brought many miles from Elis, Greece, where the games began more than 2,700 years ago. The athletes march into the stadium behind their national flag.

Derek Redmond was one of those Olympians who entered the stadium for the 1992 summer games in Barcelona, Spain. Derek, 26, had waited at least four years to compete. In Seoul, Korea, four years earlier, he had an Achilles tendon problem. He had waited until a minute and a half before the race began before he would admit to himself — he couldn't run.

In November 1990, Derek underwent operations on both Achilles' tendons. He has had five surgeries in all, but he continued to fight and came back. In fact, in the preliminary rounds he had run the 400-meter at 45.02 and 45.03, his fastest times in five years. "I really wanted to compete in my first Olympics," Redmond said. "I was feeling great." Redmond could see the finish line as he rounded the turn into the back stretch. Suddenly he felt a sharp pain go up the back of his leg. "It just came out of the blue. One minute I was running and then the next thing was a pop and I went down."

Halfway around the track Redmond lay sprawled across lane five, his right hamstring gone bad. "It dawned on me I was out of the Olympic finals," he said. "I just wanted to finish the race."

Redmond struggled to his feet and began hobbling around the track in an attempt to reach the finish line. The winner of the heat, defending Olympic Champion Steve Lewis had finished and headed toward the tunnel. So had the other six runners. But . . . the last runner in the race hadn't finished. He continued to run.

Jim Redmond, sitting high in the stands, saw Derek collapse. "You don't need accreditation in an emergency," Redmond said. So Redmond, a 49-year-old machine shop owner, ran down the steps and onto the track. The Olympic games have the security of thousands of policemen and metal detectors. But no venue is safe when a father sees his son's dream drifting away as Jim Redmond had. "I had to get to him."

The crowd, realizing that Derek Redmond

was not going to quit but rather was running the race of his life, suddenly, stood and honored him with cheers. At the final turn, Jim Redmond caught up with his son and put his arm around him. "You don't have to do this," he told his son.

"Yes, I do," said Derek.

"Well then we're going to finish together." Derek leaning on his Dad's right shoulder with intense pain began sobbing. But together, father and son kept going. An Olympic usher attempted to escort Jim Redmond off the track. If ever a futile mission had been undertaken this was one. Derek and Jim Redmond continued arm in arm until they crossed the finish line to the roar of cheers from the Olympic stadium.

When the tears had stopped, Derek reflected on the race. "I got knocked out because I finished eighth," Derek said. *"But I finished the race."*

The race results beside Redmond's name read "AB" for abandoned. However, Eric surely knows, along with a watching world, that he was not abandoned but held up and carried across the finish line by a caring and loving father. What more can we know and expect from our Heavenly Father — a true encourager.

The men who are lifting the
world upward and onward
are those who encourage more
than criticize.

— Elisabeth Harrison

See You in Nome

In the spring of 1977, when most 16-year-old boys were dreaming about a new car, Karl Clauson had a different mode of transportation in mind. His transportation didn't have horsepower but rather dog power. For you see, Karl and his family lived in the great state of Alaska. Unlike most of us, Karl and his teenage friends dreamed about when they could participate in the legendary Iditarod.

Most of us have heard about this annual event held each March, but very few really know what takes place in one of America's last frontiers. Race teams of dogs and mushers challenge each other over the grueling Alaskan terrain. Each year approximately 75 teams compete, covering some 1,150 miles from Anchorage to Nome, with many dropping out or being disqualified during the typical 11-day race. The ability to complete the entire trail is a major accomplishment.

The Iditarod was named for an old supply route to the interior of Alaska's gold mining regions. In 1925 this route was used to relay critically needed serum from Nenana to Nome during an outbreak of diphtheria. It was this dramatic run that inspired the annual "Iditarod Trail Sled Dog Race."

It was this race which young Karl Clauson began to dream about. It wasn't unusual for Karl to think about this race, but what took place in the next two years was much more than a dream. He began to take steps toward entering the race himself. He started training dogs, and for the next two years he became singularly focused and vigorously trained for the challenge that lay ahead. He worked and acquired more dogs, bought the best food, and prepared the best diet possible for his team of dogs.

Finally, after two years, he was ready. On March 5, 1979, Karl Clauson, 18, became the youngest person ever to attempt the Iditarod alone.

As Karl went to the starting line, he knew this was it. His team was prepared and they had several thousand miles of training behind them. They were in incredible shape, yet this was not a practice run on familiar ground, but the grueling trail that had caused many to stop and return, never completing the full journey.

Karl shares this word picture as an encouragement to you and me:

At the end of the starting line as I looked around at all those other teams, I could hear them discussing options, contingency plans, questions. This was going on all around me everywhere. People were saying, "Hey, what do we do if we get to McGrath or just to Ugashik? What if we get down on dogs or run out of food? How will we get back?" People twice my age and experience were making contingency plans all over the place.

Do you know what happened then? My Dad walked up to me at the front of the sled and I'll never forget this. He stuck out his hand, he looked me in the eyes and I think he had a tear or two . . . the only words he said were, "SEE YOU IN NOME!"

For the next 21 days, I went through sub-zero weather with chill factors off the chart. I got myself in dangerous situations around open water and mountain ranges. I found myself sleeping on the Yukon River with a rope tied around me and the sled.

Finally, because of extreme circumstances, I had to cover the last 450 miles of the race by myself. I had no team to run with. I got into blizzards along the Bering Sea coast and went through some unbelievable storms. Twenty-one days, 12 hours, 8 minutes, and 31 seconds later, I rounded Cape Nome and went underneath the burrow. I made it!! I made it because of powerful words that were spoken to me by my dad. "SEE YOU IN NOME!" You see, it wasn't until two years later that it ever occurred to me that I might not make it.

Now those are powerful words!

This story, shared by Karl Clauson in 1995 at Fellowship Bible Church, Little Rock, Arkansas, was the seed-planting catalyst for this book.
Thanks, Karl!

Part V

The Art of
Encouraging Words

Words have the power to persuade . . . which can be healing for eternity.

— Kenneth Parlin

An Effective Encourager

After months of dealing with an ongoing problem that just would not go away, I found myself sitting in the conference room on the 18th floor looking west toward the skyline. I could see the scenic beauty of the Arkansas River and the Arkansas State Capitol. It was a beautiful day. But . . . I wasn't here for the view. I had come to visit my friend and board chairman, Mike Haigh, who for the past seven years had encouraged me when all I could see was the discouraging side of things. He was my Barnabas (son of encouragement).

As I sat waiting in this conference room, Mike soon entered in his winsome way. It seemed as though all that really mattered to Mike was my welfare. I began to share with him my heartache and struggles as I faced a difficult time in my ministry. I explained how discouraged I was at the opposition I was facing. All of a sudden I saw Mike sit up straight and look me in the eyes and begin to quote (what I later found out was from Teddy Roosevelt) with a stirring passion that I had never seen from Mike before:

It is not the critic who counts. Not the man who points out how the strong man stumbles, or how the doer of deeds could have done them better. The credit belongs to the man who is actually in the arena, whose face is marred by dust and sweat and blood, who strives valiantly, who errs and comes short again and again because there is not effort without error and shortcoming, but who actually strives to do the deed, who spends himself on a worthy cause, who knows the great enthusiasms — the great devotions, who knows, at the best, the triumph of high achievement. And who knows, at the worst, if he fails, at least he fails while daring greatly. So that his place shall never be with those cold and timid souls who know neither victory nor defeat.

"Wow! When and why did you memorize that?" I asked Mike.

"I always admired what it said and resolved to commit it to memory," he replied.

That day as I walked out of that 18th-floor conference room I was not only encouraged by Mike's words but his commitment to shape lives for Christ in the midst of difficult circumstances. This was definitely "man-to-man" encouragement. I had once again been encouraged by Mike's intentional and sensitive style.

Later, I received this note from Mike:

> Just a quick note of encourage-
> ment. You are doing a wonderful job. I
> truly believe that there could not possi-
> bly be a better man for Ozark than you.
> I praise God for you, Jan, and the boys.
>
> Mike

I share this story to illustrate the six steps necessary to be an effective encourager.

1. *Be a cheerleader!* Most of us are avid sports fans who invest money, time, and energy into cheering our favorite teams to victory. The home team always enjoys this enthusiastic encouragement. The presence of people who feel like we do helps to bring the best out in us. Cheering is important to the success of a player (friend).

2. *Be intentional!* Most of us live such busy lives that we simply don't notice others' needs. It takes thoughtful time and energy to be a true encourager. It doesn't come naturally. Being an encourager requires intentionality. We need to recognize we are called to be encouragers, to build each other up, to bear one another's burdens, and to yes — sacrifice.

3. *Be simple!* Encouragement is not doing for someone what they can do for themselves. Rather, encouragement is the opportunity to openly

express praise for a job well-done and compliments for the value of their service. Mark Twain remarked that he could live two months on one good compliment. Positive feedback is a wonderful encouragement. A word of encouragement written or spoken is like "honeycomb sweet to the soul and healing to the bones" (Prov. 16:24).

4. *Be sensitive!* An encourager's response must be well-timed and suited to the circumstances. Sensitivity requires a real awareness of situations and a basic knowledge of how people feel in different circumstances. Be sensitive to the time, place, and environment. All of these play a vital role in creating the right atmosphere. In the words of Solomon, "Like apples of gold in settings of silver is a word spoken in right circumstances" (Prov. 25:11).

5. *Be transparent!* It's our nature to think that successful people have never made mistakes but that is not true. As people face their own challenges and failures, the simple act of being vulnerable and sharing personal examples of struggles creates on openness in the communication process. Someone facing difficulty needs to be reminded of the challenges and failures that hurt us all. Such encouragement to know God's grace is sufficient.

6. *Be available!* Encouragement is simple. Just make yourself available. Take a look around. There

is a world of needs out there. Pick someone out . . . then give them your best. Dr. F.B Meyer said it best: "If I had my ministry over again, I would devote far more time to the ministry of comfort and encouragement."

Be available to the opportunities the Lord gives us to encourage those all around us.

How many people **STOP** *because so few say* **GO**?

——*Charles R. Swindoll*

Keys to Encouragement

Make a list of people you come in contact with daily. Start with your family, co-workers, clients, neighbors, and church family. Expand your list as you become aware of special people and their needs. Daily, ask yourself "Who can I encourage today?"

Look for opportunities to write a note of encouragement, make a call, give a word of encouragement. Enjoy opportunities to celebrate others' successes. Pray for those you know need encouragement but are unwilling to receive your words.

Observe what's going on in the lives of people around you. Keep looking, asking, and noticing. Ask yourself what word would encourage them. Don't become overwhelmed at the abundance of needs, hurts, and opportunities around you. Do what you can, when you can, where you can — however you can.

Kind words can be short and easy to speak, but their echoes are truly endless.

—Mother Teresa

Don't Forget Who You Are

> But you are a chosen race, a
> royal priesthood, a holy nation, a
> people for God's own possession, that
> you may proclaim the excellence of
> Him who has called you out of dark-
> ness into His marvelous light: for you
> once were not a people, but now you
> are the people of God: you had not
> received mercy, but now you have re-
> ceived mercy (1Pet. 2:9–10).

Fred Craddock, retired professor of
preaching at Emory, was still teaching on the
faculty of Phillips University in Enid, Oklahoma, when he and his wife took a vacation in
Gatlinburg, Tennessee.

One night as they were sitting in the old
Blackberry Inn in Gatlinburg having dinner, they
noticed that an old man who appeared to be the
proprietor of the inn was moving from table to
table speaking with the guests. Now Dr.
Craddock is a rather private person, particularly
when he's on vacation, and didn't want to be

bothered. He and his wife, Nettie, were enjoying the evening. The last thing they wanted was some old stranger bothering them.

But out of the corner of his eye, the old man spotted the Craddocks and headed for their table. "Where are ya'll from?"

Craddock, hardly lifting his eyes from his meal answered tersely, "Oklahoma."

"What do you do there in Oklahoma?"

Craddock said, "I teach homiletics in the Graduate School of Phillips University," hoping the old boy wouldn't know what homiletics meant and leave them alone!

But instead he said, "Oh, so you're a preacher, are you? Well, have I got a preacher story for you!"

He began, "You see that mountain over there? I was born just a few miles from there. My mother wasn't married at the time, and the shame and reproach that fell on her fell on me as well. They had a name for me when I started to school, and it wasn't a very nice name. I remember going off by myself at recess because the other kids used to taunt me so. But the worst was to go with Mom to town on Saturday to do the shopping. All those piercing eyes staring at us, wondering, *Whose boy is he? I wonder who his father is.*

Continuing, he said, "When I was about 12 a new preacher came to our little church, and people began to talk about church again. Folks who hadn't been to church for years started coming to hear this man preach. I went myself, though I slipped in late and sat near the back for fear someone would spot me and say, "What's a boy like you doing in a place like this?"

But one Sunday the benediction got said quicker than I realized, and I found myself caught in a sea of people heading for the front door. I was terrified, scared to death someone would recognize me and embarrass me right there in church. I'd almost made it when I felt a hand on my shoulder. I turned around, and there he was, that preacher, staring at me with those burning eyes. Then he said it: "Son, who are you? I don't think I've seen you here before." And I thought to myself, *Oh no. Here we go again.*

But then a smile of recognition broke across his face, and he said, "Wait a minute! I know you! I know who you are! Why, I can see the family resemblance. You . . . you are a son of God!" Then he slapped me across the rump and said, "Boy, you come from quite a family, and you've got an inheritance. Why don't you go out there and claim it!"

Then the old man said, "You know, that one statement literally changed my whole life."

Well, by that time, Craddock was enthralled with this strange old man, and so he asked him, "Who are you, anyway?" And the man said, "My name is Hooper — Ben Hooper."

"Ben Hooper?" Craddock said. "Why I'm from Tennessee and my granddaddy used to talk about the fact that on two separate occasions the people of Tennessee elected an illegitimate to be governor, and his name was Ben Hooper! Are you he?"

"The very one!"

I believe one of the greatest needs in our day is encouragement.

— Bill Wellons

Encouraging Words

1. Great!
2. You've got it.
3. You're on the right track now.
4. That's right.
5. Unbelievable!
6. Now you have the hang of it.
7. That a way!
8. You're doing just fine.
9. Now you have it!
10. You did it!
11. Fantastic!
12. Tremendous!
13. Terrific!
14. Wow!
15. Awesome!
16. How did you do that?
17. That's better.
18. Excellent!
19. That's the best you've ever done.
20. Keep it up.
21. That's so nice.
22. Keep up the good work.
23. Good job!
24. Much better.
25. Super!
26. Exactly.
27. You make it look so easy.

28. You can do it.
29. Way to go!
30. You're doing better.
31. Superb!
32. Wonderful!
33. You're the best!
34. No one does it better.
35. You're better every day.
36. I knew you could do it.
37. Keep working on it.
38. Beautiful!
39. The best!
40. Keep it up.
41. Nothing can stop you now.
42. You're great!
43. You made me proud.
44. You did that well.
45. That's it.
46. You're learning fast.
47. Perfect.
48. Fine.
49. Congratulations!
50. Outstanding!
51. Neat.
52. Remarkable!
53. Super Star!
54. Nice work!
55. Now you're flying!
56. Bravo!
57. Hooray for you!

58. You're on target.
59. How nice.
60. Hot Dog!
61. Dynamite!
62. You're jazzed!
63. I like you.
64. Spectacular!
65. Great discovery.
66. Hip Hip Hurray!
67. Bingo!
68. Marvelous!
69. Phenomenal!
70. Exceptional Performance!
71. A real trooper.
72. What a good listener.
73. You care.
74. I trust you.
75. You mean a lot to me.
76. You make me happy.
77. A+ job!
78. You're a joy.
79. A O.K.!
80. I like that smile.
81. Keep looking up.
82. Just perfect.
83. You're important.
84. Unbelievable!
85. How did you do that?
86. You're my friend.
87. You made my day!

88. The best!
89. You discovered the secret.
90. You're a darling.
91. Kudos!
92. I like the way you work.
93. Now that's a handshake!
94. You're beautiful!
95. I'm proud of you!
96. Hurray for you!
97. You're unique.
98. What a winner!
99. You know the secret.
100. I sure do love you.

The deepest principle in human nature is the craving to be appreciated.

— William James

Share Your Encouraging Words

Contact: Ken Sutterfield
                Ozark Conference Center
                4 Ozark Mountain Road
                Solgohachia, AR 72156

                1-800-935-CAMP

Ken Sutterfield, is the executive director of Ozark Conference Center. He lives just north of Morrilton, Arkansas, with his wife, Jan, and two sons, Ragan and Spencer. This is his second book.